MY
AFMERICA

My Afmerica

Poems by Artress Bethany White

2018 Trio Award Winner

White, Artress Bethany
1st edition.

ISBN: 978-1-9494870-0-8
Library of Congress Control Number: 2018951422

Interior Layout & Cover Design by Lea C. Deschenes
Cover Art: "Daydreams or Delusions" by Stefanie Jackson
Editing by Drew S. Cook and Gabrielle Lawrence

Printed in Tennessee, USA
Trio House Press, Inc.
Ponte Vedra Beach, FL

To contact the author, send an email to tayveneese@gmail.com.

TABLE OF CONTENTS

I.

II.

I.

Plantation Wedding

I.
In the middle of my lecture
      on antebellum plantation life
                  abolition
                  Lydia Maria Child
                  and William Lloyd Garrison
pronged slave collars hung
      with iron Christmas bells ringing
                  and Kara Walker's oeuvre
                  a recasting of slavery
                  for the next generation
I finally vocalize a question
      I've suppressed

                  while binge-watching episodes
                  of *Say Yes to the Dress*

An inquiry prompted
      by southern belles

                  with visions of Scarlett
                  dancing through their heads
                  modeling some confection
                  like the curtain dress
                  admired by Rhett
Why
      would any woman

                  stage her twenty-first century
                  wedding on a plantation
                  where masters slaked their lust
                  on the shivering bodies
                  of black boys and girls?

Out in the fields
    blood seeps
        from cowhided backs
        shouldering rough cotton sacks
        the ghosts of slaves
        silent and watching

II.

Tourist-worthy quarters of whitewashed boards

fireplace more than a century cold

I revolve in a circle before a pared down slave's memory

this one-room cabin too authentic for packaging

III.
After the war,

the [slaves] left the old plantation

one by one

until there wasn't but one person in sight:

~~master~~ sitting in a wicker chair

in the yard looking out

over a field of cotton and corn

IV.
Come, experience

The oldest of love affairs

under Spanish moss

        Wedding packages

        on the sweet home plantation

        start at our nation

An American Moor in Spain

Motherland is as tangible
as the blackness of skin
and the kink of a lock
of burnished hair
under an Iberian sun.

This to a German child
visiting Spain seems to say it all:
You're African. His words stated
so emphatically after assuring him
I am American that I can
feel the annoyance
blossom in my chest
and tighten my jaw.

How to navigate this moment
when a child professes to know
more than me about who I am
as his mother stands behind
clasping small shoulders to her womb,
daring me to contradict
her son's Teutonic intellect.
Her smirk saying go ahead,
deny your continent, your birthright.

My nativity was cultivated
in the breast milk
of a native-born mother,
resting in the sinews of her progeny,
as precise an articulation as
lips to breast, hand over heart
an unshakable pledge of fealty.

This is not treason;
I am an American, though black.
I am stolen goods
but can trace my family back
three hundred years on U.S. soil,
longer than Whitman's leaves of grass,
longer than this anger will last
as I walk away muttering
I am an American.

THE UNMAKING OF BIANCA ROBERSON

Madness is a mall trip   ending in a bullet's flight.
Flight without a fight   her tombstone wedged in dust.
Dust to dust is anguish   dividing parents and their pride.
Pride is one less kid   decides the tiger on a ride.
Lanes explode in hate   a cat reaches for his stripes.
Striped ribbons of blood   wing a girl grimly skyward.
Trees choke a dad lost   in the woods of his child's death.
Death drives a pickup   full of sinister making.
Making it, making it   a mother and father labor
                    until
              their daughter
             suddenly
              stops.

ABECEDARIAN FOR PEACE

Accept that I have penned another elegy.
Besieged, the dead occupy my brain.
Comfort reigns in words on a page, a
Descant to lift the pain.
Etched into memory are names, a
Flood of American blood.
Grasping each day like a lifeline, I beg
Humanity to realign and
Inspire the gun to empty,
Just not into another body.

Kindred, I say consider peace.
Lofty goals can birth kindness in times of crisis.
Meet eyes to pass the love,
Not the hate that elongates days.
Opine carefully and
Perform lead, not bit parts. Pause before
Questioning civil rights, and I might not
Retaliate with a litany to halt a
Shrug at another lost life.
Trudge through history and stumble
Upon reflection. Pause to name the fallen.
Validate the battlefield and let
Wisdom decry the damage done. Come, explore this
Xyst of the mind with me; a garden holding the day's tally.
Yowl a refusal to wall our brethren and hear the
Zither play while we mend the broken.

African American Primer

I.   Ode to a Twenty-first Century Confederate

Camouflage baseball cap
Confederate flag stitched to the side of the backpack
The trouble you have meeting my gaze
all tell me much of what I need to know
while your classmates supply the rest.
Rich details of your bucolic hometown
where blacks are few and diversity challenged
in anti-Obama rants around the living room;
a rehearsal perhaps for the failed *coup d'etat*
in the hallway outside my class,
where you dub me a revolutionary
Spewing black rhetoric
for pricey college credit
like post-race is a place called Dixie
where integration never happened.

II.   Rebel Yell

Enough to make the heart buck in the chest.
A high-pitched scream unleashed as the car aims
for the body. Some atavistic trait
passed down for the sole purpose of shouting
Black skin, crawl back to Africa! if but
for a moment. Terse microaggression
declaring nothing less than our parents
really should have known better than to move
to suburbia, which looked and smelled safe,
a whiff of affirmatively faulty
advertising to keep black numbers small:
microscopic to the point of dismissal,
until announcing a sure 'nuf sighting
with a malevolent old rebel call.

III.   A Meditation on the Segregated Church Hour

Today, upright in another black church
      speaking in tongues as my husband sits
quietly Presbyterian alongside my hip
      longing for a hymn evoking WASP and home.
When it comes, the sermon about the state of black men
      not the *Love & Hip Hop* variety my spouse deifies
hoping one day to run into Stevie J.
      playa to dude because he has major game,
no, something more dire
      that sounds like an obit, yet appended to a reminder
to try a black jesus who may not remain silent.

IV.   Keening Latinate

A sound ancient as dirt   *terra*   solid earth
severs the ties between a mother
and her fallen boy   *filius*   a son
A primal howl paralleling the birth scream
clamo   that flung him into this world
mundus meus   my world
Oh, reverse reverberation   *echo*   unstoppable sound
anguish of a parent   *mater*   dear mother
forced to bury her child   *infans*   her baby boy
If only this final iteration   *iteratio*   speakable sound
could be transformed to prayer   *oratio*   oration
what would it say? An urgent appeal
like god if you only knew   *intellexerunt*   understood
how much he despised red ants   *formicae*   fanged /aents/
their domed hamlets made of sand
harenam   sifted grains
the wrath of their venomous stings
talis dolor   oh, such pain
you would not insist   *postulant*   demand
I lay him in the ground today
ad meridiem   at midday
alone to bear it.

MISSISSIPPI IN JUNE

for James Craig Anderson

For school children
it is a first long word,
spelling Miss-iss-ippi over and over
like a state song committed to memory.
All kinds of things are passed
down to generations by rote,
both the good and the bad,
but there is no rhyme to teach
how to mourn the death of a child
run down like road kill
for being black.

Slow down for a rabbit, raccoon
or a fox by reflex, watch
the glassy eyes of the innocent
stare into headlights,
a stunned moment
between life and death,
before compassion
presses a foot to the brake.
Religion's do unto others as you
would have them do unto you,
whether animal or man,
confirming it was not
god's workmanship
that killed your boy.

Born in 1963,
he was still a lap baby in June
when Chaney, Schwerner, and Goodman
were found dead
near a town named Philadelphia
that had nothing to do with liberty.
On that day you leaned down to kiss
the top of his head,
baby hair softly curling
under your lips,
believing in your heart
this child would inherit a better life
than Mississippi in 1964.
You were wrong.
Today, watching the videotape
of your son's last seconds on earth
raw footage
black and white
cars, people, headlights
and him holding up hands
before the bumper
dragged him from view.

In these moments
you try to work up the meanest
curse you can think of
against the injustice of it all,
but the only word
that keeps coming to mind
is Mississippi.

THE WORRY

I cringe when my white stepson
exaggerates a Southern twang,
racialized diphthongs in my brain

as he laughingly plays hillbilly,
igniting my worry over how
and when affectation can change a heart.

I worry about a house
where a man tries to parent a racist son
who once hid his hate away, now ripe

enough to meet light of day;
no more hooding of the eyes
to pantomime happy family lies.

I worry it will be me someday
my son drives under the bumper of his car,
like a final destination to *our* family situation.

TRANSRACIAL ADOPTION

Blood is thicker than water
                     which is not running
through these veins
                     but is something
less than blood kin
                     which is adoption.
I want to claim this one fully,
                     but every time I search her face
looking for something
                     that resembles my lips
the shape of my nose
                     the color of my eyes
I am mistaken,
                     and a stranger looks back at me.
My higher self,
                     intellect and not genomes,
chose this child
                     signed, sealed, and received
to raise up
                     to bring me water
to lay me in the ground
                     to spread my name
throughout eternity,
                     and yet I still forget
sometimes
                     the sharing of blood
is not the last word
                     in motherhood.
Surely it is something
                     other than an umbilical cord
knotting this union together.

THE BALLAD OF LITTLE ROSA

When liberalism
arrests you in the aisle
you never see it coming
from the lips of your mixed child,

scolding her white father
for acting just like the bus driver
demanding Rosa Parks give up her seat
after you request she stand to her feet.

To vacate the couch a journey too great
following a weary day of school,
so she morphs into Rosa the legend,
an effective educational tool.

When next you're at the playground
her afro puffs sway in the breeze
around a knot of brown children
as cute as you please.

Not budging when you beckon
to clarify this essential parental lesson,
shoes scuff sand as she eyes you with a grin
watching you call her name again and again.

Everything Resides in a Name

The day the white babysitter
calls you colored, you believe
your birth parents were rainbows,
unicorns, brightly hued fairies
dancing across the television screen—
all beautiful, colorful things.

You ask if I like being called black,
a term rich in value and tincture.
I don't mind, I say, explaining the word
is synonymous with African American,
a color awash in continental drift.

Your question, in turn, reminds me
of Alain Locke's "The New Negro"
and the student who, after reading it,
decided all blacks were Negroes again.
The label a litany through his essay I graded.

They can't keep changing their name
insists the woman who transposes the phrase
people of color to colored people.
Her refusal to keep it straight
offensive in so many ways.

Which brings me back
to the little white boy
who called you black
on the playground today,
after pushing you roughly away.

COILS

Daughter,
    your hair will govern your life
        is what I think
            but do not say,
                like integration spelled
                    the end of black hair secrets
                    long before Chris Rock
                    and the film *Good Hair*
                        spilled the dirt.
                        Yet, pondering
                        what you will say
                    when classmates ask
                How does your hair
                do that?
            and hoping for something
          witty like
      It is an act of God,
    or *Genetic sleight of hand,*
or *You would have to walk a mile*
in these hairpins
to understand.

II.
Please,
let it not be a Caucasian boy
swinging a noose through a
suburban high school door
one Halloween morn.
Robed in white,
coiled
knot
draped
along the floor,
transporting his black classmate
out of the North
where who knew
white sheets could be donned
and no one speak a word
against the hatred they condoned.
The hallowed pleats
of Old Glory
yet crackling
on a breeze
in the New England schoolyard
still declaring justice for the free.

Life as a Blonde

My daughter proudly
            delivers a paper figure
yellow yarn for hair
            Mommy, this is you,
displaying my doppelganger,
            seductive cultural snare.
I pause to consider the latest *CSI*
            myself victim of a killer
sharpening his knives
            Why are you doing this? I sob
mascara pooling beneath
            my Pecola blue eyes,
then running through the woods,
            a chainsaw nipping at my heels
until I trip on a tree root
            and the roar of the saw
is the last thing I hear.
            So, too quickly, I say
Baby, I have black yarn here
            certain life does not end well
for little black girls who imagine
            sporting blonde hair.

ROLE REVERSAL

for Sandra Bland

The cruiser makes a tight u-turn on a rural highway,
the Illinois plate reminding him of a visit to Chicago's
Navy Pier on a day so windy he felt the hawk peck the skin
of his features like a knife, but today just wants to relive
the sojourn with someone who will know what he means
when he says, well, cold. And say after relief brightens
Sandra's untroubled brown face, she tells the cop
about the job luring her from Chicago
back to this southwestern place, and he swells with pride
pleasure unwinding in his voice while stating with a bow
Welcome back to Texas, I sure hope you enjoy us now.

ENDOGAMY

It should not be a matter of endogamy,
letting race determine your mate for life.
As girls we ponder the shade of his eyes,
shape of a nose, a dome's sculpted majesty
sure genetic preference leads to matrimonial bliss.
It is not, however, the iridescence of an iris
that will forsake its health to enfold your fevered body.
Nor the Roman nose for which you search
that will ensure night after night of wild abandon
chased by I don't care who hears us.
No, it will be something much more delicious
than the texture of his hair
making you peep breathlessly
around the bathroom door
to catch a glimpse of his naked buttocks
as he undresses for the night.

Just Another History Lesson

Marriage delivers two stepsons, whose corn-silk
    manes morph into Elvis-style bed head
    neither care to tame.

I pump love from a can, wielding mousse
    like a miracle halo circling crowns. Edge
    sideburns and bangs with a rattail comb.

The boys await their turn, mesmerized
    as their black sisters rail
    against parts carved through shiny oiled hair.

Then labor suddenly turns to history in a blink,
    and I see cotton bolls stropping black fingers
    creeping up to washing clothes,

now bodies chased by bullets, endless American woes.
    No, I never whisper acculturation
    watching their eyes widen as I wield a comb.

Notes from the State of Tennessee

The woman staring
    at us now mourns our racial
        conundrum, stepson.

Inexact fear poised
    between her peeled back eyelids.
        Shock, a tight-lipped thought.

No tutorial
    prepared me to raise you here,
        a white Southern boy.

Tongue-tied, she stutters
    on eugenics and reason.
        Old Plantation tales.

Truth blooms like cotton
    in spring as sweat drips beneath
        a stranger's dismay.

Going Home

The dream of leave-taking,
never as sweet as the actual leaving.
No more explaining how this Southern town
leaches like calcium sucked from bones,
the bending near to breaking.
Think desert. Think lonesome wolf howls.
Hollow goodbyes echo empty
even to my own ears. A nose
opens in anticipation of home,
the scent of years beckoning.
I airplane arms and run
up the interstate of my mind
like a toddler convinced
lanes can fit into an embrace.
I settle for hugging trees,
nuzzle leaves and recall
childhood in a pinetum of peace,
the spice notes of conifers
begging, begging
to be swallowed again.

Aubade:
On the Pennsylvania Turnpike

I drive northwest into a dark
eclipsed by rising
    pale blue light
    above broken bodies
                of deer below.
Their tails once flicked in frolic,
    now trapped
in medias res
on asphalt.
Mountains rear beside butterscotch
               and off-white corpses
I leave behind.
So sweet in repose,
I hesitate
      to call them dead.

II.

Today a Fingertip
Hovers Over Send

Yesterday seventeen people died
and my finger hovers over send,
the button standing between one
mourner's moan and another.
I have penned an elegy for a relative
137 years after the fact and hesitate
to elide wet blood with dry.

Nonetheless, my finger descends
igniting a chain reaction. My heart's beat linked
with hundreds of others like an emphatic hive
buzzing along with my story dumped
into notifications. I catch you
dawdling over a cigarette, sitting on a couch
too old and saggy in the center for company,
wrapped in a towel, hair dripping after a shower
under knocking prewar pipes, over a hoagie
dripping vinegar beneath knuckles
and a keypad already dotted with crumbs
from other meals snatched on the run.
I want to whisper wait and see judgment
pause before descending decisively
over my thoughts charted in script,
the exoskeleton of language
revealing more than I may be ready for.

After A Daughter's Phone Call Detailing the Suicide of Another Mother's Son

A carefree, tousled-haired boy
takes his life in the most spectacular of ways,
a swan song heard round your world.

Memories of friendship a seductive susurration,
a shell overflowing with the breath of waves
now rippling through a lifeless boy's hair.

Kinship eddies beneath the bridge where we stand
under the white and yellow petals of our memorial stems.
Your world a stolen song beneath a river's churn.

He kisses air: wings extend then fold to fins
plashing beneath the water's opaque stare.
A tousled-haired end to the unruliest of days.

The gods know that no way out
is undetermined by race or creed
or songs beyond the range of this world.

One day a mother's child is here then gone,
a plea that someone, somehow, must heed.
A once carefree boy disappears,
his full-throated trill never heard again.

Taberna del Caballo / Horse Tavern

A small Spanish-American restaurant tucked
into a cobblestone lane in St. Augustine, Florida
suddenly reminds me of my grandmother.
I choose a Cuban sandwich from the menu
recalling it was her favorite and imagine hers
tasted something like this one of pulled pork, smoked ham,
Swiss, garlic aioli, mustard, and dill pickles
pressed into a bun.

Later, we visit the Castillo de San Marcos
and caress 323-year-old *coquina,* the stone
of cockleshells hand-molded into fortress walls
that took twenty-three years to build.
Now school children descend upon its courtyards
robust and fearless invaders unchecked.

I once attended a bilingual school
amid early waves of Cuban emigres,
led into the Spanish language with sock-puppet skits.
My beloved teacher lifting heavy ponytails
from my cheek as I drank water from the cooler at recess.
This is the day students around the nation
stage walkouts to protest gun violence, while at the Castillo
historically garbed volunteers prep the canon
for a ceremonial blast from the parapet toward the bay,
where only luxury yachts now sail.
No enemy left to fight, children merely bade
to cover ears against the inner drum's irrevocable pop.

Nationalized Violence

Once horror was the rattling pages of Stephen King's
Salem's Lot and a series of sleepless nights eclipsed by *Jaws* and
a belief in sharks enabled to swim across theater floors like
popcorn-splattered oceans without being stopped.
Then morphed into innocence blindsided by cancer's
gnarled bloom atop a friend's face, a terrible prelude
to death by AIDS. Or the stark vision of a flipped car,
a naked girl strewn like grief on the tar, bloodless though
all around her others are not. A frenzied buzz, *Is she gone?*
She might be gone. Can we cover her, regardless?

Now it's death stylized on a flat-screen. In this episode a
fist beats against panting lungs as a killer primes his victim
beneath a hook-studded beam. If this were real time, slow
seconds would taunt her realization's dawn:
someone is cooking dinner for their kids, while somewhere
I am a storehouse of respiration being killed.

Playing with Guns

We are four kids alone in a bedroom
with a purse and a gun.
Has there ever been a hiding place
a child couldn't find?
Two weigh the Saturday Night
Special in their palms,
two more afraid to touch it.
The one who might have
does not pull the trigger.

After a Brother's Death, 1946

(a blues)

A man was lodged in jail Friday shortly after midnight

I want to live forever in the heartbeat before fate
in Sonny Boy's smile, a toothy flash for being late.
Just back from Europe, alive but war-torn,
to a family grateful two boys returned unmourned.

Charged with murder after his brother had been fatally shot

I am stuck in the pulling I can't take back.
The knock on the door before I pull the rifle from the rack.
The knock on the door before I hear the knob jiggle.
The smile on his face before I pull the trigger.

The victim died soon after being taken to the county hospital

They shout, Take him to the hospital, looking at me
as if the building can work the miracle we all want to see;
the light returned to a body with power failure,
the resurrection of a soul heading to his savior.

*Sheriff's Deputies arrested two other men
in connection with the killing.*

There are no words after shooting your own brother.
No words for not knowing a gun was loaded.
Nothing said between father and son for one another.
Only tears sliding down black cheeks ungoaded.

Mourning Dress

for all of the Sandra Laings once
living in the segregated American South

In Anthony Fabian's film *Skin*, set in the era of apartheid,
an Afrikaner mother buys a yellow frock for her shy
black daughter. Giving into her desire for a store-bought
dress—more luxurious than the rest—staring back through
her open closet door. Thoughts still full of a mannequin
white, sleek, and slim wearing satin in a shop
where her mother would never stop—her child
legally forbidden to try on what she planned to buy.
The unspoken, *How could I sell it, you understand?*
Fear of black sweat caressing a white woman's hand
too much to bear, like eyeballing a dress for size.
Too big a must, because one could cinch in
but never take out more than fabric or tradition
                                        would allow.

Too Many Ghosts

I once intuited a ghost when I tripped down
 the wide staircase of a quaint Victorian in Medford.
As I tumbled, my eyes saw his demise: a seemingly permanent
     plank disappeared like decades beneath my tread, and I
     caught the somatic whisper, I died here, in midair. Years
     later in Salem, I tour the cemetery in town, feeling lucky
     and ahistorical, as my stepdaughter awkwardly straddles
     Puritan burial mounds. I imagine what one might say
     upon sitting up to capture us in a steely gaze.
                    Wayward girls!
                    Pagan heathen!
Before reshuffling bones to rest again. Later when I swipe
     through photos of the day, I catch my child
leaping over plots, her smile a goblin rictus at play,
paused between the tales we weave and ghostly narration.

FAMILY PLANNING

Creating good memories for a child
is a primer for sound parenting.
Deferential as the fresh scent
of a baby's breath while nestled
in the crook of a new mother's neck.
Consider how porous the nascent mind
as it beholds the impeccable divinity
of an inchworm measuring an inch,
its green luminescence balanced
on a father's gently extended fingertip.

TRIPPING WITH DAD

i.
Just another no-fail airport trip, Dad,
as you dial the check-in gate requesting
Delta wait, enlisting your fam of six
and your best British accent to divert
their quizzical surprise and bugged out eyes
when your 'fro rounds the terminal bend.
Chiming,'Twas I who called, so let's go!
while waving our boarding passes for show.
Laughing practically through takeoff at what
would now surely get you shot for a part
in a terrorist plot. Delaying planes
to get down South for the summer visit
and leaving tense airline staff in your wake
pleading *Please, sir, do not come back this way.*

ii.
Dad, let's not come back this way I plead
as our camper clings to a snowy ridge,
edging shyly along the Poconos.
Skidding past exits and quaint motels held
captive in family vacation hell,
because we owned a camper, room on wheels,
no need to stop, KOA held our spot
only a state away. Everyone tucked
into bunks unaware death might await
in a Pennsylvania valley
beneath a fragile guardrail amid snow.
Dad clearly refusing to say blizzard
between downdrafts while holding his breath,
carting the burden of lives into day.

iii.
Carting the burden of lives into day
much simpler than early American
toilet habits demanding quick transport
of another kind, I divine, during
our journey into Old Sturbridge Village
and spying the pre-toilet wooden chair.
Just a chamber pot stashed beneath a rump,
so fumigate or flick a wrist and dump
through the window, or out the door. Arcane
the shame of aqueous mechanics,
the unhidden bedpans of life. A
weary need to be rid of daily bread,
not so removed from habits of the dead,
once living ye good olde New England way.

iv.
Living life the good old New England way,
we try to care for a black buckled shoe
choosing Plymouth Rock for a windswept crew.
Could we climb the rock? Sit on the rock?
No, only whine for lunch after the rock,
begging for lobster once tasted in Maine.
We ask Dad if there were some black people
on the Mayflower decks. No, just a lot
of people wearing black like you'd expect,
ending our romance with the colony
sprung from a rock beside which we now stood.
Later, we ate lobster, grubbing white meat
from stingy red husks of sharp tail and claw,
lost spirits more Indian than Pilgrim.

v.

In spirit more Indian than Pilgrim,
we fought cultural wars road-tripping.
Roaming the wonders of the Eastern Shore,
we forced America to be our host.
Trips are how nuclear families bond
taming children akin to devil's spawn.
Dad mapped routes, predating GPS, while
bravely grooming our malaise without rest.
We gleaned endurance those hours in a car,
yearned for a respite from backseat boredom
some midnight rest stop vending machine
to stem restless fidgeting, not knowing
we'd one day become vacation gurus,
kings and queens of low-budget voyaging.

vi.
Crown king of the low-budget voyage,
Dad struck fear in my siblings' hearts, asking
the landlubbers to step on a boat.
Risking a brisk cast away, I alone felt
he could keep us afloat. Determined chin thrust
northward amid frigid ocean spray
stinging my cheeks crossing the harbor at Boothbay,
I grip the gunwale, hull slapping furled waves.
As we propel through gray mist unchecked,
stridently calling to something within
salt water, tidal elixir of brine
chanting what better home could we find.
Open mouths like fanned gills, man and fish,
rites we, a sea people, could understand.

vii.
Rites we, a free people, can understand:
wingéd first dreams of exotic places
arrowing through cloudless skies, a rippled
fuel haze trailing in a jetliner's wake.
Each of us suddenly gliding away
to parts unknown on roaring vibrations
of expense-free mechanical thunder.
Australian outback to the beaches
of Monaco, sweet agendas jigsaw
continents and voluptuous terrain.
In clouds, rapturous silence of children.
Posed atop the lone highway's grassy knoll,
palms visor faces, creased eyes squint at sky
on another airport field trip with Dad.

THE RACE

We are the only black family in the subdivision,
and your family is the poorest. This is not a matter
of bank accounts, which we know nothing about,
but the pea-green concrete of your house
prefaced by a yard more bald than hirsute.
In an enclave of Spanish-style villas and Tudors
you stand out like the soiled bare feet
and fringe of your teenage brother's cut-off shorts.
The way he fumes, when I best him
in a road race at half his age, leaves me to consider
if it was my years or color that offended him most.
Friendship between us is as amorphous
as me never meeting your parents,
yet not defining you by the ticks we delicately pluck
from your dog's back and smash beneath rocks,
while I wonder if my parents would notice
a pilfered flea collar from our own Hartz three-pack.

Dandy Buck

Dandy (noun, adjective)
    1. A man who dresses.
  Reminds himself of a truth:
      I have value; worth.

Buck (noun)
    1. Term for black male slaves.
  Fertility rate.
      Charge to procreate.

Cotillion

Her name
Yoko
no Ono
to follow.
Iconic heroine   not of Beatles fame.

Japanese like her   but a designer by right
her destiny   cultural elision of a sabler type.

Her *raison d'etre*   to the black middle class
        a white cotillion dress

she stitched   worn amid black ladies
        paired
        with austere gents.
A label
by Yoko
adorns a debutant's nape
        pooled
        to a curtsy
        before a Morehouse man's bow.

Tar Feet

Black and viscous
I am told is what my feet bring to mind
as five taunting cousins semicircle
tan toes wriggling righteously toward center.
A privileged pallor leaving me out of sync
       years before learning
       of blacks once using
       paper-bag color tests
       to tally race quarterings.
O beleaguered brown, at neither extreme
               of the chromatic meter
               yet suddenly it
               blacker than thou.

Hugh Hefner's Castoff

Sifting through
cardboard-boxed detritus
of black bourgeois
suburban life,
just kids craving anything
that might amuse
or titillate
until we found you:
photo of a bare-breasted woman
in pink underpants
passed reverently between
four pairs of hands
agreeing it had been taken
with the family Polaroid,
the half-inch border of white
perfect for recording dates and places
sadly clear of any cataloging data.
Discarded memento, never meant
for the family photo album,
but there you were
exquisitely posed
on paisley satin
without your glasses,
myopic squint
silently demurring
That is not me
as we stared knowingly
into each other's eyes
not buying the lie, Mom,
because, heck,
we'd recognize you anywhere.

The Empty Nest Dream

White tulips splayed in crystal vase
                centered on smudgeless glass table
surrounded by white leather couches
                on beautifully woven rug
dominated by white.
                This is the land of no children,
promise to self after long years
                chiseling away baby fat
primed for a passion
                not governed by magic moments
of Play-doh, bedtime stories
                first readers, squeaky music lessons
and tireless Saturdays of craft after craft
                munching peanut butter and jelly
staring into space wondering
                what the hell hit me.
Years of secret planning
                only to discover
a fly in the balm
                at the end of my mothering.
O sweet sons and daughters I carried
                and watched jettison from my womb
into the grasp of a midwife
                why do you state so adamantly now
that you will never have children
                of your own or leave home?
You are proof
                there is such a thing
as mothering too well, I think,
                while still searching doggedly
for my elusive white aviary,
                a quiet place to nest anew.

Sunday Swine

Pungent steam
hissing
from pressure cooker's
rattling top
marking time
for a meal
we know too well
though no one watches
you dress
the pig's feet
ears
and innards
we vow
never to prepare
as adults,
cementing our oath
in table play
behind your back
galloping
boiled pig hooves
across the tabletop,
mocking the meal
with scant regard
for America's
slave history
or what it meant
to live high on the hog,
and the coffled dreams of those
who made *haute cuisine*
out of the offal,
living low
on the blessèd swine.

Notes

Section III. of the poem "Plantation Wedding" is based on Image 88 from the Federal Writers Project: Slave Narrative Project, vol. 1, Alabama, Aarons-Young.

Bianca Roberson was an 18-year-old African American girl fatally shot in the head while driving on a Pennsylvania highway after an alleged road-rage incident with a white male driver in the summer of 2017.

On a June morning in 2011, James Craig Anderson was beaten and run over in Jackson, Mississippi by a group of white teenagers driving a utility vehicle. His death was captured on a surveillance camera and ruled a hate crime. It was a June day in 1964 when the civil rights workers James Chaney, Michael Schwerner, and Andrew Goodman were gunned down near Philadelphia, Mississippi. Despite the more than fifty years separating these crimes, there is still something about Mississippi in June.

One of the young men responsible for the death of James Craig Anderson "came from a mixed-race family, with a black stepfather and stepsister, and mixed cousins." (USA Today)

The phrase "seventeen people died" in the poem "Today a Fingertip Hovers Over Send" is a reference to the February 14, 2018 shooting at Marjory Stoneman Douglas High School in Parkland, Florida. The elegy referenced is one written for a relative lynched in 1881.

ACKNOWLEDGEMENTS

The author acknowledges the following journals, which first published versions of select poems from this collection:

Solstice Literary Magazine: "Plantation Wedding"

Pleiades: "Everything Resides in a Name"

The Account: "An American Moor in Spain" and "Role Reversal"

Poet Lore: "Playing With Guns"

Menacing Hedge: "Sunday Swine"

The New Guard: "Mississippi in June" (finalist for the 2015 Knightville Poetry Contest)

Sin Fronteras/Writers Without Borders: "Adoption" (now "Transracial Adoption")

Mud Season Review: "Hugh Hefner's Castoff," "Coils," and "Conversation With Daughter" (now "Endogamy")

Special Thanks

I would be remiss in not thanking the dedicated hands that went into making this book a reality. I would like to thank Sun Yung Shin for her astute reading of my manuscript as a contest judge and Gabrielle Lawrence and Drew S. Cook for their essential editorial suggestions and support through the production process of this volume. I would also like to thank Tayve Neese for her timely handling of the business side of things. Additional thanks to The Writer's Hotel, the Sewanee Writers' Conference, and Tupelo Press /MASS MoCA Residency for providing the space, time, and funding where early and later versions of these poems were lovingly workshopped. Poets must be heard, so I would also like to thank the following reading series and venues for giving me pre-publication space to share my work: Random Name Poetry Series, Philadelphia, PA; Rosemont College MFA Reading Series; Bowery Poetry Club hosted by The Writers Hotel, New York, NY; Monday Night Poetry and Music at East Bay Meeting House, Charleston, SC; the Burlington Writers Workshop; the Association of Writers and Writing Programs. I would also like to thank my family, especially my husband, for their consistent support. Finally, if I neglected to mention anyone who supported me through this process due to human error, I apologize for the omission and thank you.

ABOUT THE AUTHOR

Artress Bethany White is a poet, essayist, literary critic and the author of *Fast Fat Girls In Pink Hot Pants* (2012), a collection of poetry. More recent poetry has appeared in such journals as *Poet Lore, Ecotone, The Account, Pleiades,* and *Solstice.* White earned a master's degree in creative writing from New York University and a Ph.D. from the University of Kentucky. She is a visiting assistant professor of American cultural studies at Albright College in Pennsylvania. She has received The Mona Van Duyn Scholarship in Poetry from the Sewanee Writers' Conference, the Mary Hambidge Distinguished Fellowship from the Hambidge Center for Creative Arts for her nonfiction, and a writing residency scholarship at the Tupelo Press/MASS MoCA studios. Previous prose appears in *Blood Orange Review.* New essays, "Sonny Boy" and "A Lynching in North Carolina," appear in *The Hopkins Review* and *Tupelo Quarterly.* Her most recent literary/cultural criticism, "Appalachian Literature and Race Relations in the Newer South: Homogeneity and History in Ron Rash's *Burning Bright* and Natasha Trethewey's *Native Guard,*" appears in *Seeking Home: Marginalization and Representation in Appalachian Literature and Song* (University of Tennessee Press, 2017). Her chapter examines how contemporary writers are providing new ways to talk about the history of the Civil War in the wake of continued debates on the legacy of the Confederacy. Previous scholarship, "From Africa to America By Way of the Caribbean: Fictionalized Histories of the Diasporic Slave Woman's Presence in America in *I, Tituba, Black Witch of Salem* and *A Mercy*" appears in *Literary Expressions of African Spirituality* (Lexington Books, 2013).

About the Artist

Cover Art: "Daydreams or Delusions" by Stefanie Jackson (courtesy of the artist)

Stefanie Jackson is an Associate Professor of Art at the Lamar Dodd School of Art, University of Georgia, where she teaches undergraduate and graduate drawing and painting. Jackson is the recipient of several prestigious awards, most recently the 2017 Anonymous Was A Woman Award. She has received several individual grants from the Georgia Council for the Arts and a Special Projects Grant from the National Endowment of the Arts. Jackson's paintings are in the collection of the Georgia Museum of Art, Birmingham Museum of Art, Larry and Brenda Thompson Collection of African American Art, the Kerry and C. Betty Davis Collection, the Clark Atlanta University Art Galleries, and The Detroit Institute of Arts.

About the Book

My Afmerica was designed at Trio House Press through the collaboration of:

Drew S. Cook, Lead Editor
Gabrielle Lawrence, Supporting Editor
Lea C. Deschenes, Interior Design & Cover Design
"Daydreams or Delusions" by Stefanie Jackson, Cover Art

The text is set in Adobe Caslon Pro.

The publication of this book is made possible, whole or in part,
by the generous support of the following individuals and/or agencies:

Anonymous

About the Press

Trio House Press is a collective press. Individuals within our organization come together and are motivated by the primary shared goal of publishing distinct American voices in poetry. All THP published poets must agree to serve as Collective Members of the Trio House Press for twenty-four months after publication in order to assist with the press and bring more Trio books into print. Award winners and published poets must serve on one of four committees: Production and Design, Distribution and Sales, Educational Development, or Fundraising and Marketing. Our Collective Members reside in cities from New York to San Francisco.

Trio House Press adheres to and supports all ethical standards and guidelines outlined by the CLMP.

Trio House Press, Inc., is dedicated to the promotion of poetry as literary art, which enhances the human experience and its culture. We contribute in an innovative and distinct way to American Poetry by publishing emerging and established poets, providing educational materials, and fostering the artistic process of writing poetry. For further information, or to consider making a donation to Trio House Press, please visit us online at: www.triohousepress.org.

Other Trio House Press Books you might enjoy:

Two Towns Over by Darren C. Demaree
    2017 Trio Award Winner selected by Campbell McGrath

Bird~Brain by Matt Mauch, 2017

Dark Tussock Moth by Mary Cisper
    2016 Trio Award Winner selected by Bhisham Bherwani

Break the Habit by Tara Betts, 2016

Bone Music by Stephen Cramer
    2015 Louise Bogan Award selected by Kimiko Hahn

*Rigging a Chevy into a Time Machine and Other Ways
    to Escape a Plague* by Carolyn Hembree
    2015 Trio Award Winner selected by Neil Shepard

Magpies in the Valley of Oleanders by Kyle McCord, 2015

Your Immaculate Heart by Annmarie O'Connell, 2015

The Alchemy of My Mortal Form by Sandy Longhorn
    2014 Louise Bogan Winner selected by Carol Frost

What the Night Numbered by Bradford Tice
    2014 Trio Award Winner selected by Peter Campion

Flight of August by Lawrence Eby
    2013 Louise Bogan Winner selected by Joan Houlihan

The Consolations by John W. Evans
    2013 Trio Award Winner selected by Mihaela Moscaliuc

Fellow Odd Fellow by Steven Riel, 2013

Clay by David Groff
    2012 Louise Bogan Winner selected by Michael Waters

Gold Passage by Iris Jamahl Dunkle
    2012 Trio Award Winner selected by Ross Gay

If You're Lucky Is a Theory of Mine by Matt Mauch, 2012

CPSIA information can be obtained
at www.ICGtesting.com
Printed in the USA
BVHW030501310119
539085BV00001B/6/P

9 781949 487008